Then, And After

Poems Between Memories and Becoming....

Parul Patet

BookLeaf Publishing

India | USA | UK

Made with ❤ on the BookLeaf Publishing Platform

www.bookleafpub.in

www.bookleafpub.com

Dedication

To my parents, for their unwavering support,
To my sister, for always pushing me to do more,
To Siddhant and Dhruv, you both are my reason in life,
To Bua, for always being there,
And
To a new community for guiding me on a difficult
journey I have undertaken.

Preface

When I started writing these poems, there was no clear theme or idea in my mind. I just knew that I wanted to say something that had been germinating inside for too long.

Whether it was listening to my elders tell stories from their past, looking at old photo albums of my childhood, or just something that crossed my mind for a fleeting moment. There were things to be said.

I am not a poet, not by a long shot, but I have been made aware that things can change in an instant, and don't want to wait anymore. So, I take this as an opportunity to share snapshots of my life which has been touched by grey skies as well as golden sunshine.

These are the voices in my head that have started to become coherent...at last!

Acknowledgements

This collection is a reflection of moments—some fleeting, some enduring—that have shaped who I am. Every memory woven into these poems carries the imprint of people, places, and experiences that have left their mark on my heart.

I am deeply grateful to my family, whose presence in my life has given me the memories worth writing about. Your love, support, and stories have been both my comfort and my inspiration.

Lastly, every poem in this book is a reflection of lived moments, emotions, and truths. To life itself—thank you for being the raw material of art.

1. Memories from 10, Krishan Nagar: Poem 1

Who lived here first?
Four brothers and two sisters.
Who looked after them?
They looked after themselves,
Grew up quickly, too quickly
Teaching, learning, quarrelling, cajoling, encouraging,
supporting, laughing and crying
with each other.

Was it difficult?
It was not easy; but they had hope ... and each other.
Laughter and happiness were found
in cups of hot tea, impromptu picnics, make- believe
wrestling matches,
Bicycle rides and daily chores.

And so they grew up.

Were they happy?

The eldest sister devoted her life to care of her siblings...
she was happy.
The eldest brother started working as soon as he could
....he was happy.
The younger sister postponed her dream of higher
studies for a job..... she was happy.
And
The other three brothers worked hard to achieve their
dreams,
To keep the faith alive
To make the sacrifices count
To make everything better for everyone.... They were
happy.

Who lived here first?
A family that is still one.
After children
After grandchildren
After successes, and failures
After numerous ups and downs,
A family lives here.

2. Memories from 10, Krishan Nagar: Poem 2

Do you see that sprawling house with the large blue gate,
A tall eucalyptus tree, standing guard near the entrance?
That is my home, my refuge and my safe haven.

All old houses look the same, you say.
Look closely....
Can you see the bougainvillea hedge bursting with crimson?
It calls out good cheer to the passing wind, fluttering and swaying with joy.
Can you see the crooked guava tree in the corner?
Its fruit-laden branches whisper to the neighbourhood children to come and enjoy.
Can you see the windows shining with light?
They beckon passers-by to come and rest after a day of toil and employ.

All old houses are the same, you say.

Listen closely......
Can you hear the laughter of the eight cousins playing around?
They brighten the large courtyard, running and shouting, catching imaginary foes.
Can you hear them calling out to the other children to join?
For the house is where everyone comes together, to talk or plan, standing close.

The eight cousins put up plays and skits,
Whether scenes from the Ramayana, or self-written comedies
that are watched by parents and neighbours sitting on mismatched chairs.

The house witnesses it all.....
The camaraderie, the secrets told under the cloak of a summer evening,
First crushes, First successes, First disappointments, First heartbreaks....
Birthday parties, Janmasthami tableaux, Holi and Diwali celebrations, Dussehra rituals
are just a few of the highlights of the beautiful chaos seen and remembered by it.

All houses are the same, you say?

Not my house....
It still whispers the carefree joy of a childhood spent
here,
It still tells stories of adventure and togetherness so rare,
It still waits for when we all come together on special
days

Looking at us through its old eyes, and smiling, it says
'Welcome back my children.'
The house is growing old, but the memories are young
and vivid,
It's a part of me, just as I am a part of it-
A constant through all the upheavals and tribulations, it
stands defiant.

All houses are the same, you say?
Not this house, not my house,
And I thank God for it every single day.

3. Little Things of Joy

The call of the nightingale, carried on the wind,
Fills my heart with untold joy,
For it heals the day's toil and worry
Hope shines bright in my heart, and doubt is destroyed.

The sound of raindrops on the roof I hear,
Rhythm of raindrops, the melody of nature's song ,
Music for ears that have long suffered the noise and
chaos,
Lifts my heart with happiness, whispering, this is where
I belong.

The bright blue sky on a winter morn I see,
Not a speck of grey, not a hint of silvery clouds are
around,
A sight so magical, I gaze in awe and disbelief,
For such a sky only in paintings and pictures is found.

A cup of coffee and a good book to read,
Sitting in the fading evening sunlight,

Living each incident with characters as one,
Is enough to make even the dreariest of days joyful and
bright.

Little things are all we need to lift our spirits,
But we keep waiting for something momentous to
celebrate,
In doing so we miss what's right there in front,
All it takes are little things, to make a day great!

So dance in the shadows, let laughter ring clear,
Embrace every heartbeat, the small moments dear,
For life is a tapestry, woven with care,
And joy lies in the simple—the love that we share.

Look closely at flowers, how they bloom and they sway,
Each petal a treasure, embracing the day.
In the quiet of twilight, let dreams take their flight,
For every small wonder transforms dark into light.

4. A Place Called Dehra

Once Dehra was a jewel, shining green and bright and
pristine,
Nestled between the mighty ranges like a pearl, in an
ocean clean.
Home to dreamers, poets, artists, who looked for a place
of repose
Where life was slow, and sky filled with a million
rainbows.

The majestic building of F.R.I.
The tolling bells of the Clock Tower
The bustling markets famed for rice
The gushing water springs, the ancient temples, the
botanical gardens
Were but a few of the things that captured the eye,
So, one could rest their weary soul, and watch the world
go by.

Spring burst forth in a splendour of colour and
fragrance,

Gardens filled with luscious and verdant greens.
Summers temperate with the cool evening breeze,
Bringing *mangoes* and *litchis*, delicious to eat perchance.

Then came the stormy cumulus clouds, bringing rain and
life anew,
The town rejoiced with the shimmery showers, treetops
waved in an ancient dance.
Winters were cold, but bright sunshine made it cheerful
and happy,
And so ended the year, with a myriad of colours, all a
part of Nature's beautiful glance.

All that is gone now:

Traffic jams, high rise buildings, broken roads, flooded
streets, garbage dumps
have taken the place of the beauty that was.
Summers are hot and humid
Rains wreak havoc on the hills
Winters bring no joy or cheer
Things have changed, all that we held dear.

But Dehra still breathes and calls out for help,
For much can be done if we all come to the fore,

Do one little thing and pay it forward,
And return Dehra to the green jewel of yore.

5. Falling Leaves

The leaves on the guava tree have turned brown and
brittle
There are no more fruits to hide
They wait, signalling the arrival of autumn,
Biding their time, the final goodbye.
Their journey started in the spring, when the tree was
thick with new-born foliage,
For long the leaves were a welcome sight
Green, soft, making the tree a beauty and treat for weary
eyes.

The leaves have played their part.
They no longer have a role , no longer a purpose or a
goal,
The end is nigh, the life is drawing to an end, their
journey done.
And so they wait....
There's no fear, no regret: for they had a good life
Which is all they could have hoped for.

They don't tremble
They don't look back
They don't cling to the tree.
For they are ready to fall to the soft earth
Where it all started.

From dust the tree rose and gave them birth,
And dust will be their final resting place.
The leaves will sink into the earth, at one with the
Mother,
And soon new seeds will spring to life and a new tree
will be born again.

The leaves never feared falling to the ground,
They just needed the right kind of wind
To carry them softly down.....
And complete the circle of their life.

6. Diary of a Forest

Day 1
The birds are fewer now
Their chirping getting fainter and fainter
Deer, elephants, bears and lions are scarce,
Dead of hunger and thirst and so much heat.
Even the bees and crickets have paused their incessant
song
As if waiting for a signal, some primitive call to reassure
them
That all is well.

Day 25
Spring is here
Flowers should be blooming, new leaves and saplings
Should be taking hold, welcoming new life in all its form.
But I am slowly turning brown, not green or emerald.
In vain do I search for signs that I have endured,
But alas, none can be found.

Day 85

I see a child look at a picture of a deer
'What is this creature?' he asks his mother.
'It was once found in the forest,' she points at me-
The child looks in awe, as if at some alien out of his
dream.
More questions are asked by him, and answered by the
mother
As best as she can.
For, she has also seen my trees, and birds, and animals,
and insects
In books, film or museums.

Day _____
The Earth is all shades of grey and brown
I exist no more.
All my creatures are extinct, humans don't recognize any
other things living,
Skyscrapers abound, gigantic planes fly, sounds and
sights of progress all around.
Seasons are gone; its just one long hot day and cold
insufferable night
Humans in their air conditioned houses sit and watch
large screens
Looking and marvelling at the beauty that was-
They look at moving pictures of me – **the forest.**

7. Beyond screens

The pavements and alleys were our playground,
And laughter and yells were happy sounds.
We didn't need batteries or electricity so we could run
Pure and simple games, played just for fun.

Hide and seek, dodgeball , 'pitthoo' and catch,
Deciding who, out of us all, had met their match.
Gully cricket, badminton, football in the street,
The neighbourhood would resonate with the sound of
our feet.

If we felt adventurous, we climbed the nearby hill
And taking a picnic there, had our fill.
A rainy afternoon was an excuse for rain –dance,
No DJ needed, nothing mattered but that wondrous
chance.

We didn't wait for joysticks or controllers to fight
imaginary foes,
For swords and arrows were made from cardboard, and

we stood in rows.
Spinning stories, using creativity at every turn,
Oh, the remarkable tales of glory and daring that were
churned!

Hopscotch squares were drawn on sidewalks and
pavements,
Just a skipping rope was enough to engage us in joyful
movement.
Waiting eagerly for the ice cream vendor's call,
This simple pleasure didn't have to wait till a trip to the
mall.

So here's a cheer to the leisure we enjoyed all day long,
The world our playground and togetherness our song.
Before the pings and continuous blue beams--
There was a time when we played games beyond screens.

8. Search for Purpose

I used to think purpose was like a mountain
Still, big and un-moving.
Something that was unchanging
Something I had to conquer and climb.

I thought purpose was a river flowing free
Meandering through the vast plains of life,
Something that followed an orderly path
Something I needed to pursue and reach in the end.

But now I have seen what is real
Mountains shift, rivers change course
And purpose, like a stream,
Can carve holes in even hard rocks.

Sometimes I'm a writer, or a teacher
Other days I fancy myself a listener and confidante.
I chase meaning like a mirage moving away,
Out of reach, like the ends of a rainbow.

I have worn a number of dreams, like leaves on a tree
But today, shedding those leaves is my purpose.
I breathe more easily
And start once more—
The older version just an image in my rear view.

For true purpose is the journey you undertake
With the people you support and who support you.
Purpose is not a moment, a point at the end of a line,
It is never ending and ever changing—
And discovering who one is, that's the greatest purpose
of all.

So I gather these moments, like drops of rain,
Each one a lesson, a heartbeat, a thread.
I weave them together into a tapestry bright,
Of laughter and tears, of paths I've tread.

No longer a climb, no longer a chase,
But a calm rhythm of now and tomorrow,
In each step, a whisper of who I can be,
Purpose blooms softly, not born of sorrow.

9. My Inheritance

I didn't ask for riches or gold
Or houses or land.
But I was given a treasure
In the form of wisdom hard earned.
Lessons of hard work, hope and faith-
Through all the ups and down –
I have learned.

My grandmother taught me the power of prayer
And I sat with her while she chanted
Her daily verses.
Grandpa's stories were funny and never-ending
But spoke of morals and good sense.

My mother-
Soft, yet with silent strength
Still guiding, still the axis of our revolving world.
Teaching the value of labours of love-
Without complaint.

My father-
A man of few words, but with rare wisdom,
Giving me the courage to hope
And dream.
A tower of strength, in storms of despair.

I used to think I had nothing.
Then realized –
I carried the values of generations with me.
The stories of survival,
The early struggles,
The faith and hope,
It's built into me, like flesh and blood.
More precious than gold
Or money, or riches untold.
For I carry the legacy of men and women
Who fail, but never give up.

10. Why I Teach

'Those who can't- teach.'

I teach not because it's just a job that pays,
Nor for any recognition or praise,
I guide young minds to be curious and confident,
So that it's their learning on which they can depend.

For that one shy student who speaks up before a crowd,
And his soft whispers now become loud.
Shaping and moulding, leading to a future bright,
Guiding learners from darkness towards knowledge and
light.

Paid with bright eyes and welcoming smiles,
A murmured "thank you" is enough to take me miles.
Greeting cards made on note book pages,
Can take away the hours of hard labour for ages.

I teach through the notes piled on my desk,
Through questions repeated and grammar tests.

I teach through the chaos, the silence, the noise,
Through losses and triumph and moments of joy.

Those who can't – teach.

I will never know where their journeys will go,
If they'll paint, build, or lead, and their calibre will show.
But I teach in the hope that one day they'll see—
Where and how far they have come, and who helped
them to be.

11. Snapshots of Happiness

I open the album
that was lying dusty in a drawer,
And past spills out
like sunlight through a window
that had been closed too long.

Pictures of my father, uncles and aunts-
black and white memories of a time gone by.
Wearing large-collared shirts and bellbottoms
Hairstyles inspired by the cinema-
They stand with arms around each other,
Faces shining with joy of togetherness

There we are—
My cousins and I.
Grinning, faces bright with mischief,
hands sticky, dressed in our best for the photo
as if we know the moment
is special.

A birthday party planned with love,
With crazy hats and a crooked cake.
Parents, relatives, friends –
all trying to cram into a small knot
For that perfect shot.

Even the awkward Rakshabandhan photos—
make me smile now.
That hair!
Those outfits!
The small arms filled with huge rakhis
as if in competition...
But oh, the childhood in those eyes.

Each photo is a celebration
of something we didn't know
we'd miss—
or something we still carry,
quiet and golden.
And as I flip each page,
I don't feel older or sad-
Just grateful for the snapshots
that hold joy
so gently in their paper frames.

12. Rain on a Tin Roof

It starts without warning—
like a soft beating of drums,
light fingers a rhythm
on the old tin roof above me.

Not music, or song, exactly—
but something older and magical.
A language only the roof remembers.
And I listen
hoping that I might understand it this time.

The rain does not hurry.
It starts and pauses,
It lets silence speak between syllables.
A slow, comfortable conversation
between sky and shade.

I sit in the dim room,
enjoying the kind of quiet

that only arrives
when the I stop asking questions that don't have
answers.

Each rain drop is like a thought
falling through the grey clouds.
It doesn't break anything,
Allowing free rein to my imagination.

Outside, the trees are drenched in it,
happy not to be still.
They know how to listen to the rain-
something I'm still learning.

The roof holds it all together—
the rain, the silence,
the music playing its own notes,
and none of these moments are forgotten.

13. The Language of Clouds

Clouds speak in curved lines and delicate threads,
In floating beasts and drifting heads.
A rabbit jumps, a bird takes flight—
then disappears into the fading light.

A warrior is seen with sword held high,
But disappears before I can say goodbye.
I can make out a face that once was known,
It becomes a hill, then then a milky stone.

They have no voice, no pen, but still they write
in an unknown language of grey and white.
A message seen for just a glance—
a fleeting picture, witnessed by chance.

The sun comes out and clouds start glowing,
Like shiny, precious dreams forever going.
I watch, I marvel, and as soon as I blink—
what I saw is lost in the evening ink.

14. A Message for the Children

Listen my children—
not with ears,
but with the hearts inside your chest
to the wind that speaks softly
through the trees you don't recognize yet.

There is no map or formula for *being*.
You are not a problem to be solved
or a competition to be won.
You are a new story being written
like the sunrise after a long night.

People will show you many mirrors—
some broken,
some too small—
but these mirrors do not know
what your whole face looks like.
You will learn to see

when you *become.*

Ask questions.
Ask them of the stars,
the trees, the noise,
the silence.
Let curiosity be your passion,
not your fear.

Kindness is not weakness.
It is the courage
to keep your hand and heart open
even when everyone around you closes theirs.

There will be days
when everything feels too heavy, too dark, too gloomy,
like even your existence is a burden—
but even then,
you are not alone, you are not defeated.

Breathe.
Begin again.
You are allowed to be unfinished
A work in progress-
As is the sky, the oceans, the earth.
As are we all.

15. Music of Spring

In the silence of dawn, the songbirds sing,
Their lyrics like threads of woven spring.
The frost retires with good grace,
Bright sunlight envelops the valley's face.

The daisies and pansies gently break the ground,
Though silence and gloom was winter's sound.
Now streams awaken with silvery flow,
While mountain peaks are still covered with snow.

The hills, silent, lost in ancient thought,
As if keeping an eye on what spring has brought.
Their stillness reminder of things long past—
And talks of sweet memories that will always last.

Beneath the earth, the roots still sleep,
In shadows, like the secrets they keep.
Yet in this slow and fragrant air,
Is a promise of something new, pure and rare.

I sit in my garden, filled with delicate perfume,
Waiting for the colourful new flowers to bloom.
And wonder if, like spring, I too
Might rise once more, but in brighter hue.

16. Hope Floats

When days are dark and heavens are grey,
And all the joy is far away,
Hope is there, like a quiet light,
That softly shines in the inky night.

It doesn't shout or wave or cheer,
But stands with us when there is something to fear.
It lives inside our silent doubts,
And through the heaviness we can hear its shouts.

Hope is small, but its promise is true—
A seed that grows when everything looks blue.
It tells us things will be okay,
These storms will pass, and sunshine will stay.

So when you feel everything caving in,
Take a breath, and let the hope begin.
It walks with you, along all the uneven roads —

And just when you are drowning, you'll see that hope floats.

17. What's in a Birthday?

The day arrives without ceremony—
no sound of trumpets or fanfare,
the same light spilling through the curtains
but just a little differently,
as if the sun, too, remembers.

Another year,
folded neatly behind you
like a dress worn often, comfortable
and kept only for sentiment.
Maybe a bit frayed and tired,
Still warm with memories and laughter.

There's no sudden wisdom
that you acquire,
or a bulb of knowledge that goes on in your brain.
Only a slow softening of attitude—
changed by the past that you have
weathered and endured.

Changed by small kindnesses,
and acts of understanding-
things you once took for granted.

People say,
"Make a wish."
But these days
you listen more
than you wish.

You think about the hands
that first held you,
Teaching you to walk and talk.
Hands that you hold now,
and the miracle in the fact
that you are all
passing through
each other's stories in the moment.

Birthdays aren't milestones,
they are not supposed to be.
They're mirrors.
They ask:
Are you becoming
someone you'd want to meet?
Or have as a friend?
Are you someone to depend on, to trust?

Are you still willing to learn something new?

The day ends as softly as it came,
like dusk,
the birthday candles go out
And you—
still wondering, still questioning
still grateful—
step into another
unwritten
page of future.

18. The Sun Comes Out

The world forgets how to be bright
until the sun returns.
After days of incessant rain and gloom,
It waits with bated breath.

The sun doesn't arrive with a sudden, golden glare,
just appears quietly
over the edge of morning.
Light spills light gently
into a world
that has been grey too long.

The trees, still damp,
Leaves glistening with precious stones,
come out from deep slumber
holding their breath—
not in fear,
but with expectation.
They have been here before:

the weight before the relief,
the dark before the silver.

Puddles slowly lose their width
and reflect the clouds
floating away on the
soft wings of breeze.

I walk out,
glad of the promises made by sunlight.
I don't know what I hope to find,
but something about the rays
filtering through the
wet leaves
makes the silence a sign
of good things to come.

I wonder if grief, too,
can be a long spell of rain—
and maybe the sun
will come out.
Not a cure,
but a friend, long awaited,
arriving late,
yet still arriving.

19. What They Teach

They speak in stories, and in deeds,
About patched-up clothes and minimal needs,
About winters cold and summers difficult,
And finding joy , and the cosy homes they built.

Their lessons aren't tied with pretty bows,
Just tales, like a mountain river that flows-
Of rusted bikes and simple treasures,
Of quiet dreams and easily found pleasures.

We listen, young, but didn't see
The knowledge, true, they spoke unknowingly—
That being strong is not always loud,
And there's dignity in being silent and proud.

They speak of schools with windows missing panes,
Of chalkboard dust and a roof that let in the rains,
Of sharing bread and having each other's back,

Of making sacrifices, not dwelling on things they lack.

Their stories are like little roads,
On a map that guides us, with secret codes.
In every tale, a hidden thread—
A way to live by what they said.

They teach us not through lecture or praise,
But how they made it through difficult days,
And still found hope, still made do—
They built a world from what they knew.

So let's all hold these stories near—
Each word, a precious truth we didn't hear,
Until we see what we didn't discuss,
They've handed down their best of *us*.

20. Breaking up - With My Pancreas

I used to revel carelessly
in hunger,
in thirst,
in my body's quiet routines.

Now I am learning
a new way of life—
numbers that rise and fall
like waves in a stormy sea I didn't ask to navigate.
Was it my fault?
Did I eat too much sugar-
Or didn't exercise?
Was I being punished for
something I'd done
to someone?

Doctors called it
a chronic condition,

but I call it
an awakening.
No time to grieve for the loss,
No time for regrets
Or asking God-
'Why me?'

I have become a student again,
learning-
To listen closer.
To tune in
to the pulse behind my ribs,
to the tremble in my hands
or the tide of weakness
before the drop.

Yes—
there is fear
still,
those cold, sharp moments
when "forever" looms
in the middle of any given moment.
I'm trying to reassure myself
that forever isn't a prison—
it's a road.
And roads will go places.

I see a different myself
in the mirror,
with lancets and meters and
eyes clear from crying.
I'm learning
to treat my body
not as broken,
but as a puzzle I solve,
every single day.

There is strength
in what I carry:
juice boxes, glucose, apple slices in my bag.
CGM beeps like an alternate heartbeat,
its sound like a beacon guiding me.
Some nights,
I curse the silence
when it hides a low,
Checking and re checking constantly.
Other nights,
I thank the science
keeping me here.

This diagnosis
did not take
my future—
It changed the future

and handed me
a sharpened vision
to see.

I know now that I must learn-
to fight,
to live deliberately,
and to bend
without breaking.

So I will rise—
again,
and again,
and again.
Not because I must,
but because
I can.

21. All I Need

I carry this burden quietly—
a machine continuously stuck inside me,
a day of pricks and calculations,
decisions
every hour
that most people never have to make.

You think you know something
because you've read an article,
Or saw a video,
because you knew someone
who had the "other kind."

But there are things you don't see:
I'm still here.
Still standing, doing my chores,
Still choosing to show up and smile
in a body that demands
everything from me.

I measure my strength
in insulin doses
and blood sugar curves.
In waking up at 3 a.m.
jolted by alarms, drenched in sweat,
with my body seconds from silence.
In learning and understanding for myself
when doctors, relatives, even friends
didn't understand.

No-
I am not broken.
I am precise.
I am disciplined.
Fighting battles each day
you can't see with your eyes.

So next time you wonder or judge me
for what I can or can't do,
remember—
I live with a body
that tests me every day.
And still I rise,
again and again.

And if you're willing to listen—

really listen—
then walk beside me.
Ask. Learn. Support.
Because all I need is empathy
not pity or judgement.